Download Gopher Lawn Care

Dedication

This book is dedicated to all those of you out there crazy enough to start your own business. You are all my heroes.

Getting a business going can be so damn tough. It is very difficult to find people to even bounce ideas off of without getting an ear full of negative responses.

"Why do you want to do that? Why don't you just get a job? Stop wasting your time with all those crazy thoughts."

The list of goofy responses one may be on the receiving end, knows no boundaries.

People will do what ever they can to dissuade you from becoming an adventurer. They will try to stop you from going out there into the void to explore. To feel around for success.

What the others don't understand is we do this because we HAVE to do it. This is what we live for.

So don't you stop. Be tenacious and never give up.

Never....

The landscaping and lawn care business plan startup guide.

A step by step guide on how to make a landscape or lawn care business plan with real life examples including income and expense projections as well as customer acquisition goals.

By Steve Low

Host of The GopherHaul Lawn Care Business Show

and the Gopher Lawn Care Business Forum.

Table Of Contents

Special thanks to Gopher Lawn Care Software.

This book would not have been possible without the help and guidance of all our friends and business owners we have met over the years on our forum as well as others. As with everything, this book is a work in progress. If you would like to contribute some of your thoughts and reflections on it, please send them to us via our forum or email support@gophersoftware.com.

Also thank you to the staff at Gopher Software for making all of this possible.

Lawn Care Software

PROBLEM: Scheduling & billing repetitive jobs is tedious and time consuming.

SOLUTION: Gopher Billing & Scheduling Software allows you to Quickly and Easily schedule jobs and create invoices.

Gopher Landscape Billing and Scheduling Software simplifies the task of scheduling your lawn care jobs and billing your customers. Simply set up your jobs at the beginning of the season and let Gopher handle the rest. With Gopher, you can print out a list of scheduled jobs for each day and then automatically print invoices after those jobs have been completed.

Download your free trial of Gopher Billing & Scheduling Software at http://www.gophersoftware.com

Continue your reading.

I have more great information on running a lawn care business in my other books, **"Stop Lowballing! A Lawn Care Business Owner's Guide To Success."**

Some of the topics discussed in the book: - How to start up your lawn care

business. - Finding your niche and finding profits. - Lawn Care Equipment. - Pricing & Estimating Lawn Care Jobs. - Dealing With Customers. - Dealing With Employees. - Lawn Care Marketing Secrets. - Lawn Care Business Tips. - Getting Commercial Accounts without commercial references. - Pitfalls of Commercial Accounts. And more.

The GopherHaul Lawn Care Marketing & Landscaping Business Show Episode Guide.

Topics discuss include: How to raise start up capital. Seasonal marketing ideas. What to do when your largest client leaves? What's better to use, postcards or brochures? How to build your customer base with referrals? Gain one customer then lose one customer. How to stop it? How to pre-qualify customers when they call? How to bid jobs. What should you include in a commercial lawn care bid? What newspaper ads work best? How to buy a lawn care business. Tips on buying used lawn care equipment. And much more.

How to get customers for your landscaping and lawn care business all year long. Volume 1.

Anyone can start a lawn care business, the tricky part is finding customers. Learn how in this book.

New lawn care business owners were polled and 33% of them said the toughest part about running their business was finding customers. This book shows you how to get new lawn care customers. Don't start from scratch and try to re-create the wheel. Learn what works and what doesn't.

Volume #1 discusses: Getting started, choosing a business name, harnessing employees to sell, community marketing ideas, free rentals to offer, hosting events to get exposure, volunteer projects to build goodwill, how to get residential and commercial customers (including sample letters). Bikini lawn care, getting in your local paper, marketing on price, publicity stunts & media attention, organic lawn care marketing, reaching out to realtors, turning hobbies into marketing ideas, seasonal marketing ideas that work.

How to get customers for your landscaping and lawn care business all year long. Volume 2.

Anyone can start a lawn care business but most get stuck finding customers and they give up their new venture too quickly. Why struggle trying to learn how to gain new lawn care customers the hard way? This book gives you lawn care marketing ideas that are being used by your competitors. It also talks about what marketing ideas don't work.

Volume #2 discusses: The most effective lawn care business marketing methods. How to track your ads, the best ways to utilize: billboards, brochures, business cards, buying lawn care customers, clubs & organizations, coupons & gift cards, co-marketing, door hangers, going door to door, flyers, internet marketing, lawn signs, customer letters, direct mailing, newsletters, newspaper ad, phone book advertising, phones & telemarketing, postcards, referrals, sports, testimonials, trade shows, truck & trailer advertising, word of mouth.

The Big Lawn Care Marketing Book

This book contains 470 pages of marketing ideas to help your lawn care & landscaping business grow.

The Big Lawn Care Marketing Book contains volume 1 & 2 of my other books "How to get customers for your landscaping and lawn care business all year long."

How to use Gopher Lawn Care Business Billing & Scheduling Software.

Learn how to manage your lawn care and landscaping business easier with this powerful software.

You can order my books through these websites.

http://www.gopherforum.com

http://www.gophersoftware.com

http://www.amazon.com

Intro

I have been interested in learning how businesses work for a long time. Some entrepreneurs are able to hit on something their first try. Some others take longer. While I think the vast majority of new business owners go into a venture knowing little about how to run the business they are starting. Sure they may know something about how to perform a specific service or task but they quickly learn that there is an entirely different skill set needed to run a business than there is to perform a specialized task.

This book is a great tool to help you improve your odds of finding success. I had helped create a business plan with each one of these new lawn care businesses showcased. What is quite fascinating about this is each one of them took a little different path towards putting together their business. Reading through each of the business plans will help you formulate your own business plan.

Once you create your business plan, compare and contrast your answers to what they answered. See if you left out some expenses that they included. Compare who your target audience is to their's or how many customers you plan on acquiring. Ask yourself if you were competing against these businesses, how would you differentiate yourself and stand out?

I hope all these examples help you. If you get stuck along the way, get on the Gopher Lawn Care Business Forum at http://www.gopherforum.com and ask what ever questions you have. Either I or a fellow forum member will be able to help you out. Also utilize the forum's search feature. There are many many great lawn care business discussions in there just waiting for you to discover them.

Sincerely, Steve

Project: Team Green Lawn Care

Project Team Green Lawn Care is a new start up lawn care business in need of direction to get themselves on the right track.

Here is their business plan.

Business Description:

> My Business will provide basic mow and blow service to the residents and businesses within my immediate area. In a market swamped with illegitimate companies with poor to non existent customer support, "My business" will stand as a role model of convenience and customer satisfaction.

Management Abilities:

> I've worked in customer service related fields. I think the service skills I've developed over the years will be <u>THE</u> skill that makes my business a success. Acquiring customers and keeping them will be my biggest strength. When an issue arises with a homeowner, my competitors view it as a problem. I view it as an opportunity. I know if I can resolve the issue and satisfy the homeowners concern, then I've just created an account that is MORE loyal to me then my standard accounts.

Business Strategy:

> My biggest opportunity is the lack of organized and

legitimate competitors. All of these local gardeners work purely from word of mouth, that means they have zero advertising exposure. The customer service is also non existent. We had a gardener serving my mother's house and I remember I had to speak to his 12 year old son and have him repeat it to the father. Tell me there isn't a need in my market that I can fill!

We plan on taking advantage of this by hitting the street. I will be knocking on doors and hanging door hangers. A mailing will also be in our near future. Being the only advertiser of gardening service should give us a quick base.

Maintaining our competitive edge will come with time. Once we are established and have our cost to a minimum, it will be difficulty for a competitor to come in a take a piece of our market share.

Our biggest strength is also our biggest challenge. Our competitor's costs are a fraction of ours. They don't pay insurance, taxes, zero advertising cost, and they hire illegal immigrants. They will offer to mow a homeowners lawn for $15 a month. That is less then we charge to mow. The answer to this is to educate the homeowner on the risks and to create a value for our clients. They have to see enough value in our service to warrant the cost.

Legal Structure:

The business will start as a sole proprietor. I am planning on moving to an llc or corp in the future but I'm still going over the pros and cons. I hear its much more complicated to sell an LLC than a corp.

Until I change from a sole proprietor, my insurance will have to cover my business exposure.

Mission Statement:

"MY business" is a lawn maintenance company that services my immediate area. We aim to provide lawn care that is convenient to the customer. Provides quality work and service at the lowest possible cost.

Marketing Slogan:

None as of yet, it will be something serviced based.

Market Analysis:

I have not followed any local or national treads in the market.

Customer Analysis:

My target customers are.....This is hard for me to say, I'm tempted to say "everyone is a potential customer." This will take some time for me to figure out. Once I'm out working and talking to potential customers, I'll learn who it is I should target and who it is I should avoid.

My customers will be located within my local area codes. We will expand to surrounding area codes once established.

My customers want convenience. They don't want to have to think about lawn care. They want it taken care of with minimal thought investment. This is why we will only bill by credit card. It saves our customers the hassle of receiving a bill, writing a check, and mailing out the payment.

Competition Analysis:

My competition consists mostly of illegitimate businesses. Very few speak English. They only offer the most basic services. There are a few others that do speak English but can only be found by word of mouth.

- Most run crews of 1 to 4 people.
- Their estimated sales volume is hard to figure. Most work lawn care part time. Most average between $10k and $20k a year.
- They all offer basic mow, trim, and blow service. Maybe some pruning, but nothing more.
- They produce average quality work.
- They price themselves between $15 and $30 a cut. Right now everyone is their customer because they have no alternative.
- Their strength's are the low overhead cost. No payroll, no insurance, etc.
- Their weaknesses include a lack of customer service, language barriers, rough and unprofessional appearances, lack of any service above basic mow and blow.
- I see them as indirect competitors. Customers are going to want more than the bare minimum will come to me.

Financial:

- I will personally invest $3,000 in cash into the business
- I will look to the bank to finance the truck $5,000.
- I'm looking for zero dollars from private investors.
- I should break even around month 5 and after that I will make profit.

Start up cost:

- Equipment = $6,940 (see below in the equipment section).
- Liability Insurance $1,200-$1,800 a year.
- Commercial truck insurance $1,200 a year.
- Business cards $75.
- Door hanger printing $300.
- Door hanger design $100.
- Business license $160.

Operating expenses:

- Gasoline $100/month.
- Monthly cell phone and business phone will run about $75/month.
- Grass dumping charge $40/month

Sales forecast:

- 5 new accounts a week, which equals 1 new account per day, Monday through Friday.
- Once I reach 100 account(should be around month 4) I will no longer mow myself but sell and run the business.

Labor:

- I will start by myself, pick up a part time guys when I'm around 20 accounts.
- 100 accounts I will have 2 part time guys doing all the work.
- I figure it will take them 67.2 hour a month to complete.
- 2 part time employees will make between $7 - $8 an hour. = $1,008 hours work per month. Add taxes and workman's comp bring the total to $1,287. (this figure doesn't include non-billable time.)

Equipment:

- 21' walk behind mower $1,100
- Line trimmer $300
- Hand Held blower $275
- Truck $5,000
- Trailer $250 (I have no idea, small trailer to only fit 2 - 21' mowers)
- flat head shovel $15
- All equipment will be stored in my garage for free.

Advertising / Promotion:

- Our business will be promoted through door hanger, and direct mailings.
- We will spend roughly $3-$4k on advertising.

Steve: "What ideas are you considering for a business market slogan?"

Mac: "Recommended by 4 out of 5 lawns."

Steve: "Can you think about the following questions?

1. A total number of customers you feel you can **easily** attract this season.
2. A total number of customers you feel will be **moderately difficult** to attract this season.
3. A total number of customers you feel will be **extremely tough** to attract this season.
4. What date do you want these total customers by?

This will help you set up some goals for your marketing campaign."

Mac: "I think for me, the hardest customers for me to get will be the **first** 20-30. I'll set a goal of 2 1/2 months for this. That will give me roughly 54 business days to attract them. That's one new customer every 1.8 days

The moderately hard ones will be 30-65. I'll give myself 2 months to achieve this. That's 1 new customer every 1.2 business days.

The easiest ones will be 65-100. I will figure one a day, so a month and 1/2 to achieve this.

I think 100 customers in very doable. 130 will be moderately difficult. 200 will be very difficult. I would want these customers in 8-9 month from my start date."

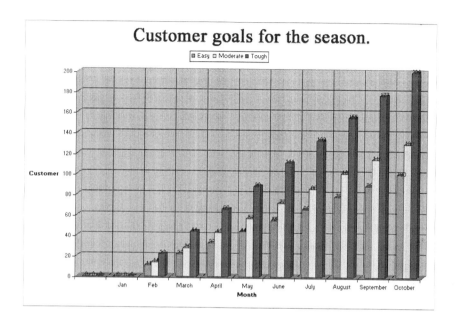

Customer goals for the season.

Steve: "Here is a chart where the vertical axis shows the number of customers and the horizontal axis shows the month. There are three bars per month showing the easiest customer goal to the moderate and then toughest."

Project: Lightning Lawn Care

Project Lightning Lawn Care is a new start up lawn care business.

Mike: "I am 20 years old. I've mowed grass for other companies since I was 16 and just started my own this past June. I now have 31 full time customers that I do on the weekend and I work a full time job during the week to make ends meet. I think I could use all the help I can get to go full time this summer."

Steve: "Mike have you filled out your business plan yet? Can we see what you have come up with?"

Mike: "Here you go."

Business Description:

Brief description.

- Lightning Lawn Care is a owner operated business that just started in June. I run a residential and commercial lawn business and currently have 30 full time accounts.

What services does your business offer?

- I offer complete lawn and landscape maintenance.

What value does it add to the marketplace?

- Not every lawn service around here does lawn and landscape maintenance so I guess it adds value that I include landscape maintenance.

Management Abilities:

What are your qualifications?

- I've done lawn work for 4 years.

How will your experience contribute to the success of your business?

- Very much, you really need to know what your doing in able to keep your customers happy with you.

Business Strategy:

What are the key strategic opportunities you have identified in your marketplace?

- A lot of new residential developments.

How will your business take advantage of these strategic opportunities more effectively than your competition?

- Provide a more professional look to the potential customers.

How do you intend to maintain your competitive edge?

- Keep doing good work.

Describe the key challenges you face and how will you overcome them?

- Adding more customers this summer by ADVERTISING!

Legal Structure:

Will your business operate as a sole proprietor, partnership, corporation or an LLC?

- Sole Proprietor

How will your legal structure decrease your business's exposure to risk?

- I don't know.

Financial:

How much will you personally invest in your business?

- So far I have invested about $11,000…I know in the future it will be much more.

How much money are you seeking from banks?

- None

How much money are you seeking from private investors?

- None

How long until you plan to break even?

- End of next year

How long until you plan on making a profit?

- After next year.

What will your start-up costs be? Be specific, describe each and the cost.

- It was $11,000

What is your sales forecast for each month of the entire year? List each month's goal.

- Right now I make about $1,600.00 each month, This year I would like to increase that number by at least $500.00 a month when the season hits.

What will be your operating expenses? Be specific, describe each and the cost.

- I figure, about $30.00 a day in gas, $500.00 a year in maintenance to my machines, edger blades, oil, string, etc..

What will your fixed costs be? Be specific, describe each and the cost.

- I'm not sure what fixed costs are?

Mission Statement:

What is your business?

- A Lawn and Landscape Maintenance Company

How will your business succeed?

- With good work.

What values are important to your business?

- Making the customer happy.

How does your business improve the lives of your customers' and employees'?

- My customers get to enjoy a beautiful lawn with no effort.

Marketing Slogan:
What is your marketing slogan?

- We'll Be There in a Flash!!

Market Analysis:

What are the positive NATIONAL trends that will affect your business?

- Growing economy

What are the negative NATIONAL trends that will affect your business?

- High gas prices.

How will you take advantage of the positive trends and deal with the negative trends?

- Add more customers in order to make up for the gas prices.

What are the positive REGIONAL trends that will affect your business?

- Not sure.

What are the negative REGIONAL trends that will affect your business?

- Not sure.

How will you take advantage of the positive trends and deal with the negative trends?

- Not Sure.

What are the positive LANDSCAPE INDUSTRY trends that will affect your business?

- Better equipment every year.

What are the negative LANDSCAPE INDUSTRY trends that will

affect your business?

- Low ballers. Competitors who are not insured.

How will you take advantage of the positive trends and deal with the negative trends?

- Buy better equipment, do better work than the other guy.

Customer Analysis:

Who are your target customers? (age range, education level, occupations, average home value)

- Most are elderly customers that are unable to do the work, other than that everyone is a target customer to me.

What do your customers want?

- Quality work, at reasonable prices.

Competition Analysis:

Who are your competitors?

- Other lawn services.

How many employees do they have?

- Varies from none to numerous crews.

What is their estimated sales volume?

- Any where from what I make to probably close to 1 million.

What services do they offer?

- Lawn and Landscape maintenance, Landscape installation, spraying and fertilizing.

What is the quality of their product?

- Poor to Excellent.

What is the price range of their product?

- From $15 a cut and up or $50 a month and up

Who are there customers?

- All ranges

What are their strengths?

- Good equipment

What are their weaknesses?

- Unreliable help

Are they a direct or indirect competitor?

- Indirect I think, there is so much work to be done around here.

Labor:

How many employees will you start with? Full or p/t?

- None, just myself.

What will the hourly labor wage paid to employees be?

- I think I'll start my first employee out a probably $8.00 an hour and depending on how good he is raise it up accordingly.

What will your total annual labor hours be?

- 40-50 hours a week from March to Oct. 20 hours a week from Nov.-Feb.

Equipment:

What equipment will be needed?

- A 52 stander, another blower and weed wacker.

How much will it cost to obtain this equipment?

- Probably around $8,000

Where will you store the equipment?

- In my garage.

How much will it cost to store the equipment?

- Free

Advertising / Promotion:

How will you advertise or promote your business?

- Flyers, business cards, yellow page ad, newspaper ad, word of mouth.

How much will you spend doing each per year?

- $2,000.

Steve: "In your business plan you said you weren't sure what fixed costs were. Fixed costs are expenses such as rent, insurance, interest on loans, etc. They don't change regardless if your production increases or decreases."

Mike: "Ok my fixed costs I believe are:

1- 36" stander - $200.00/month.

$2,000.00 Loan for:

- 1 weed eater
- 1 blower
- 1 edger
- 1 hedge trimmer
- Multiple Hand Tools, shovels, rakes, etc.
  Lawn Trailer

Insurance - $100.00/mth.

Business License - $35.00/yr.
Business Phone - $140.00/month.
Internet - $40.00/month.

My truck is paid for, but it's a dodge dakota that has almost 200,000 miles on it and only has a V6 so I will be getting a new truck when I get about 60 monthly yards total.
I will also get another lawn mower when I gain more yards.
I do not have business insurance yet, but I will. Not sure of the cost of that."

Steve: "I see you have 31 full time customers that you service on the weekends. What I would also like to see is this.

Three projections:

> 1. A total number of new customers you feel you can **easily** attract this season.
> 2. A total number of new customers you feel will be **moderately difficult** to attract this season.
> 3. A total number of new customers you feel will be **extremely tough** to attract this season.
> 4. What date do you want these total customers by?"

Mike: "A total number of new customers you feel you can easily attract this season.

- 15-20 monthly accounts.

A total number of new customers you feel will be moderately difficult to attract this season.

- 30-40 monthly accounts.

A total number of new customers you feel will be extremely tough to attract this season.

- 50-60 monthly accounts

What date do you want these total customers by?

- End of October, or beginning of November. That's when we go to our every other week schedule."

Steve: "Here is a chart to show your customer goals for this season.

The easy goal is charted to attain the lower level of your easy goal, 15 new customers.

The moderately difficult goal is charted to attain the middle of your moderately difficult goal, 35 new customers.

The extremely tough goal is charted to attain the high end of your extremely tough goal, 60 new customers."

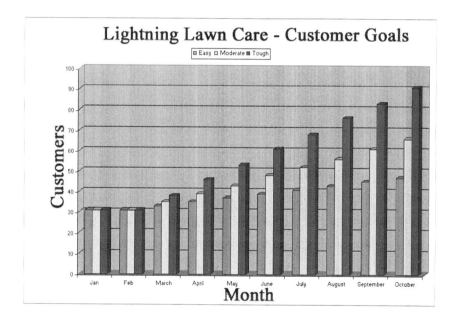

Steve: "What is the monthly fee to pay off the equipment $2,000.00 loan?

How much do you want to make after taxes per hour?

How many billable hours do you plan on working **each month** of this year?"

Mike: "I just sold a dirtbike, and when I deposit the check I will mail my final payment and it will be paid off this month. It was $120.00/month for the $2,000.00 equipment loan.

How much do you want to make after taxes per hour?
40-60 $/hr.

How many billable hours do you plan on working each month of this year? It all depends on how many accounts I gain each month. But I'll make a projection.

Jan total billable hours = 32
Feb =32
Mar = 32
Apr = 96
May = 96
Jun = 128
Jul = 128
Aug = 160
Sept = 160
Oct = 160
Nov = 80
Dec = 80

Yearly total billable hours = 1,184 (estimated) it's probably going to be more, but thats on the low end."

Steve: "This information will help you figure out how much your monthly expenses. Then you can see with your billable hours, how much you need to be making.

Next thing you should do is figure out which zip code area you want to service and do an online search at a place like ESRI Business Solutions

http://reports.esribis.com/esribis?command=zipcodelookup
and see which zip code area has the highest median income.

	ZIP 32926	ZIP 32927	ZIP 32780	National
Total Population	21,184	29,210	32,354	295,628,353
Total Households	8,335	9,624	14,364	111,572,974
Median Household Income	$45,226.00	$49,78.00	$43,225.00	$48,124.00
HH Income Under $50K	56.40%	50.40%	56.80%	51.70%
HH Income $50K-$100K	31.70%	39.60%	30.10%	31.00%
HH Income Over $100K	11.90%	10.10%	13.20%	17.40%
Average Home Value	$127,077.00	$115,771.00	$135,368.00	$206,430.00
Median Age	39.7	35	43.3	
% older than 62	14.10%	9.20%	22.30%	

Find the highest median age, the highest property value and the highest % of incomes over $100,000.00. Then hit that area the hardest with your marketing material."

Mike: "Yes, that's a good idea. I have about half my accounts out in that area. I just recently put an ad in two different newspapers in that area as well. My ad said **Lawn Service, Quality work at an affordable price, Free Estimates** and in the other paper I advertise in, I had an 1/8 page ad that pretty much said the same thing, but had my company name on it and my slogan. I also had some yard signs made up."

April update:

Mike: "I just wanted to update on my monthly accounts that I have. I have 46 monthly accounts, and I keep getting calls every week. I am currently advertising in 1 newspaper, 1 community magazine, Yellow Page ad, and I have several signs posted in my yards all over my area. Hopefully this continues for several more months. I recently bought a new truck from the added income the new yards gained me. So everything is going well. Thanks for all your help."

Steve: "That is fantastic news. If we look at your chart, you are well ahead of where you wanted to be for the month of April as far as customer count. It's amazing how creating a battle plan can really help your business grow."

June update:

Mike: "As of today I am up to 54 accounts that are on a monthly service agreement. I am not full time yet, but I could be if I wanted I work Thurs. Fri. and Sat. cutting grass. I hope to be full time by the end of the summer with at least 80 accounts which would be at the tough mark on my customer goal chart. Thanks for all your help."

Project: Sherry Landscaping

Business Description:

Sherry Landscaping is a landscaping business, specializing in lawn and garden maintenance. Building our reputation for high quality and personal attention throughout our surrounding area. We offer service to suit your budget. At Sherry Landscaping we work hard with you to bring your lawn and garden to life with quality service. Our goal is for the homeowner and commercial customer to enjoy every moment they spend in or look at their lawn and garden.

Management:

I have worked in the service field since graduating high school a few years ago. This requires a high level of customer service and quality work to earn a good reputation. I know the quality of our work is determined by the effort and skill I put into it, this is why every job no matter how big or small is a personal challenge. This will all play a big role in the success of Sherry Landscaping.

Business Strategy:

Sherry Landscaping will be targeting residential homes in low to mid income areas. This is a market that is in need of a quality lawn care provider in this area. We will also target small business accounts that typically consist of banks, gas stations and small office parks. These are customers that are in high demand and require a significant amount of work as well as snow plowing. We will maintain quality work, a professional image, and provide an image that our customers will be proud of. Sherry Landscaping will be starting a full force marketing campaign that will send us flying for spring.

Legal Structure:

The company is currently set up as a sole proprietorship. I will be working this season on forming a Corporation, or an LLC.

Financial:

As of this date I have invested about $46,000 in the form of a truck and equipment. I consider this price minimal for the amount of opportunity it provides. I will be seeking a small amount of capital from a bank for the advertising campaign. This will be my start up cost.

The monthly operating expenses are are as follows:

- Gas: $200.00
- Maintenance of equipment $50.00
- Regular Advertising: $100.00
- Office Supplies: $50.00

The monthly fixed costs are:

- Truck: $570.00
- Insurance: $218.00
- Bus. Insurance: $96.00
- Plow: 120.00
- Phone, Internet: $90.00
- Cell: $70.00

Mission Statement:

Sherry Landscaping is a full service lawn care company. We strive to keep each and every customer happy. We provide are customers with a beautiful lawn at an affordable price.

Current Slogan:

"Quality Work, Affordable Price."

Market Analysis:

National:

The Internet has become a valuable asset to many of us, as it has been to our industry. With more and more people accessing the Internet are market becomes stronger. This leaves are potential customers some time to easily squeeze in an email at the office, check out are services, and make a decision if they would like to have us come out and speak with them.

The gas prices have spun out of control and that adds to any business overhead. This in return drives prices up and suddenly we do not sound so affordable. The way we deal with this is to have a specific market that we will do all our advertising in. This will keep all of our customers in one area, which leads to less travel time and keeps our pricing competitive.

Regional:

Due to the high rise of home ownership in my area there are more potential customers. These are customers that are new to homeownership and excited about getting their lawn in shape.

On the other side of the coin the pricing of homeownership is at an all time high. This leaves potential customers on a tighter budget. To deal with this we offer affordable prices and take away the hassle of lawn care after a long day at work. This in return gives are customers a beautiful lawn and more time to enjoy it.

Landscape Industry:

More and more people have become interested in having a nicely maintained lawn. This gives us a stronger market.

There are a lot of people starting a landscape company to make some extra cash. This in return makes it harder for us to stay competitive due to overhead. I do not feel this is a big hurdle if handled correctly. I will take them around their yard and explain what they will receive from Sherry Landscaping for the price quoted. The quality of our work and the personal attention my customers receive will keep them coming.

Customer Analysis:

Our target customers are generally low to mid income homeowners. These would be customers that work a full time job or just have little time for lawn care. We are going to gear our efforts toward target areas that meet these guidelines. We will be servicing 3 zip code areas and surrounding towns. At Sherry Landscaping we know that quality is as important as an affordable price, and that's what we strive for.

Competition Analysis:

There are a few main competitors in my area. They go from a one-crew operation to a multi crew operation and produce numbers from $100k – $500k and upwards per season. They offer lawn care, install, and chemicals. I have done some research on the quality of work in my area and find in a lot of cases the better the quality gets the less personal attention the customer gets. The price ranges are $35 and up per cut, and $45 and up per fertilizing. Their customers range in all different areas. There main strengths seem to be new equipment and having the capital needed for advertising. There main weakness is there ability to balance quality work and customer relationships. These will be both direct and indirect competitors.

Labor:

I will be doing this full time and have people ready to work once I am ready for them. I am hoping to have work for 2 employees this season. The hourly wage will be based on experience and job description. The amount of man hours will be determined by the level of business I attract.

Equipment:

I have all equipment needed right now. Other equipment purchases will be minor until company expansion. All equipment will be stored in a garage at my residence.

- new 03 f350 dump truck
- new trailer
- used 52" ferris walk behind
- used 16hp giant vac
- new trimmers and blowers

Advertising:

We will be promoting our business through mailings, fliers, door hangers, business cards, and customer referrals. Amount spent will be determined by our success.

Steve: "Great job on the business plan so far. Can you give me some projections as to how many customers you will be shooting for this year?

> 1. A total number of new customers you feel you can **easily** attract this season.
>
> 2. A total number of new customers you feel will be **moderately difficult** to attract this season.
>
> 3. A total number of new customers you feel will be **extremely tough** to attract this season.
>
> 4. What date do you want these total customers by?"

Sherry: "When I started I was working for a contractor that was doing general maintenance on 28 housing units for a company. They needed a landscaper so I bid on it and landed it. Bought my equipment and never looked back. I worked full time as a contractor then part time on the landscaping. I was very busy and did not attack new work (big mistake). Now I am left with only 7 accounts because the contractor lost the account with the company. Which means I lost the account with him. I tried to get it from the company direct but my old contract would not allow this. So all my eggs where in one basket. Now I am working to

build it back up this year.
Here are the three projections:

1. A total number of new customers you feel you can easily attract this season.

- I would say 20 - 30

2. A total number of new customers you feel will be moderately difficult to attract this season.

- I would say 30 - 40

3. A total number of new customers you feel will be extremely tough to attract this season.

- I would say 40+

4. What date do you want these total customers by?

- I would like the total customer base by the end of September."

Steve: "Here is a customer goal chart for this year ending in August to help motivate you. Now that we have these goals, you will be able to chart your progress throughout the season and compare where you are to where you want to be.

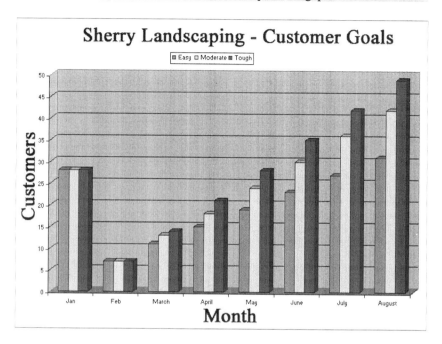

Here is another chart showing your monthly expenses. As of this date $46,000.00 has been invested into the company in the form of a truck and equipment.

Break even point. **None of this includes a salary to you.**
$1564.00 / 21 = $74.47 This is your monthly expenses divided by the average number of workdays per month which we have figured to be 21. This brings us to $74.47 per day in expenses.

$74.47 / 8 = $9.30 per hour expenses.

The next thing you should consider is **how much do you want to pay yourself per hour.** Then your salary can be factored in. Also consider what will your expenses be per hour for your salary in the form of taxes?"

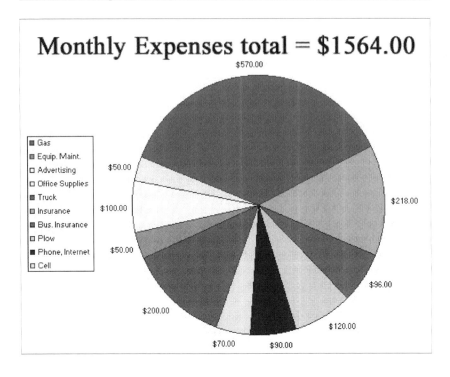

Here is a customer analysis based on zip codes you provided. The yellow highlights point out the zip code with the highest average home value and median household income. You will notice in one zip code that 44% of the households have income over $100,000.00 a year vs. another which has only 16% of the households making over $100,000.00 a year.

You may want to consider targeting the richer areas because those are the ones who have the where with all to pay for a well maintained lawn.

	ZIP 82401	ZIP 87601	ZIP 85101	National
Total Population	25,057	29,129	29,235	295,628,353
Total Households	9,348	10,181	10,029	111,572,974
Median Household Income	$90,288.00	$83,556.00	$50,641.00	$48,124.00
HH Income Under $50K	23.80%	23.70%	49.20%	51.70%
HH Income $50K-$100K	31.60%	37.40%	34.40%	31.00%
HH Income Over $100K	44.60%	38.90%	16.40%	17.40%
Average Home Value	$364,715.00	$328,173.00	$221,456.00	$206,430.00
Median Age	38.9			
% older than 62	15.80%			

Sherry: "I would like to be making $35 per hour. So I have to factor that into my monthly expenses plus taxes."

Steve: "How many billable hours do you plan on working **each month** of this year?"

Sherry: "Here we go....

Jan = 50 billable hours
Feb = 50
Mar = 160
Apr =160
May = 160
Jun = 160
Jul = 160
Aug = 160
Sept = 160
Oct = 160
Nov = 50
Dec = 50

Yearly total = 1480"

Matt: "Here are some rough accounting and tax information figures based on your company's goal of billing $35.00 per hour for 1480 hours annually and using your expenses. Just use these as a guideline and don't take them as an absolute.

Based on an income of $51,800 and expenses totally $18,768 The profit from the business would be $33,062.

Based on this income level taking a standard deduction and assuming the taxpayer is single with no dependents they would owe the following in taxes

Federal would be $3,051
Self-employment taxes would be $4,667
Your state's income tax would be at a base rate of 5.3% net of deductions approximately $950"

Project: Custom Care Landscaping

Jeff: "Hi all, my name is Jeff, the name of my company is Custom Care Landscaping. I am 25 yrs old and this year will be my first full year full time. I already have all of the equipment needed and truck. I have 8 years experience in the field working for a large company and decided it was time to go out on my own. I could really use some help with my business planning.

Here is what I have been able to put together thus far for my business plan.

Business Description:

Custom Care Landscaping is a family owned and operated company. We currently have 15 signed contracts of both commercial and residential customers. The company will stand out as a quality company and not quantity.

What services does your business offer?

- Lawn Maintenance
- Mulch/ Bed edging
- Minor Tree work
- Design Install
- Retaining Walls
- Aerate / Overseeding
- Spring/ Fall clean-ups
- Planting
- Fertilization
- Snow management

What value does your business add to the market place?

- We provide a one stop for all of your lawn and landscaping needs. Convenient monthly billing, pay as you go or 12 month. Family owned and operated.

Management Abilities:

What are your qualifications?

- I have worked in this field for 10 yrs. I have worked in all the areas of this field.

How will your experience contribute to the success of your business?

- While working for a few companies I have learned what to do and what not to do. I have also learned how to work smarter and more efficient.

Business Strategy:

What are the key strategic opportunities you have identified in your marketplace?

- The area I live right by is one of the fastest growing areas in the U.S. Having all English speaking employees working for the company is important to always maintaining good communication between us and the customers.

How will your business take advantage of these strategic opportunities more effectively than your competition?

- Provide the costumers with a program tailored to their needs.

How do you intend to maintain your competitive edge?

- Have the latest technology in all of my equipment, to be more productive and efficient. Also to be prompt and professional looking.

Describe the key challenges you face and how will you overcome them?

- To have a enough work to keep us busy 5 - 6 days a week. We will do this by advertising and bidding aggressively.

Legal Structure:

Will your business operate as a sole proprietor, partnership, corporation or an LLC?

- Corporation

How will your legal structure decrease your business's exposure to risk?

- I am not sure.

Financial:

How much will you personally invest in your business?

- $0

How much money are you seeking from banks?

- $0

How much money are you seeking from private investors?

- $0

How long until you plan to break even?

- By May of this year.

How long until you plan on making a profit?

- May of this year.

What will your start-up costs be? Be specific, describe each and the cost.

- Everything is already started.

What is your sales forecast for each month of the entire year? List each month's goal.

- $8,000.00

What will be your operating expenses? Be specific, describe each and the cost.

- Gas $ 800
- Maintenance $500

What will your fixed costs be? Be specific, describe each and the cost.

- Insurance $2,500 per year
- salaries $4,000 per month
- phone $200 per month
- taxes
- advertising $2,000 yellow pages and internet per year

Mission Statement:

What is your business?

- Lawn and Landscape Service

How will your business succeed?

- By offering clients programs and quality services that fit their needs.

What values are important to your business?

- Customers and Professionalism

How does your business improve the lives of your customers' and employees'?

- By providing more leisure time for clients and providing employees with great pay.

Marketing Slogan:

What is your marketing slogan?

- "Big enough to get you you business... small enough to

keep it."

Market Analysis:

What are the positive NATIONAL trends that will affect your business?

- More people buying homes today than ever before.

What are the negative NATIONAL trends that will affect your business?

- More and more people are losing their jobs to over seas.

How will you take advantage of the positive trends and deal with the negative trends?

- By targeting advertising in new developments.

What are the positive REGIONAL trends that will affect your business?

- More and more people acquiring ownership of homes.

What are the negative REGIONAL trends that will affect your business?

- People losing their jobs.

How will you take advantage of the positive trends and deal with the negative trends?

- Advertise and offer an affordable but not cheap service.

What are the positive LANDSCAPE INDUSTRY trends that will affect your business?

- More and more people are hiring lawn care professionals.

What are the negative LANDSCAPE INDUSTRY trends that will affect your business?

- The prices of equipment and steel are on the rise. The emissions of 2 cycle equipment. The insurance costs going up every year.

How will you take advantage of the positive trends and deal with the negative trends?

- Build up my clientèle to compensate for the rising prices of doing business.

Customer Analysis:

Who are your target customers? (age range, education level, occupations, average home value)

- 30 + years old. Some college and up. It really doesn't matter on occupation. Income of $150,000 +

What zip codes do they live in?

What do your customers want?

- Quality lawn care.

Competition Analysis:

Who are your competitors?

- Lawn care companies with 1 - 2 crews

How many employees do they have?

- 2 - 4

What is their estimated sales volume?

- $150,000

What services do they offer?

Mowing, fertilization, mulch , and lawn maintenance.

What is the quality of their product?

- Not the best.

What is the price range of their product?

- $40- 60 per cut.

Who are there customers?

- I don't know.

What are their strengths?

- Size.

What are their weaknesses?

- No commitment to quality or on time services.

Are they a direct or indirect competitor?

- Direct

Labor:

How many employees will you start with? Full or p/t?

- 2 full time (including myself.)

What will the hourly labor wage paid to employees be?

- $10

What will your total annual labor hours be?

- 1,500 hours

Equipment:

What equipment will be needed?

- None I have all of it. Here is a list.
- 2000 GMC Sierra 4x4
- 60" Exmark Turf Tracer 23 kaw ecs
- 52" Exmark Turf Tracer
- 32" Emark Metro
- 2 Redmax weed eaters
- 1 Redmax straight shaft stick edger
- 1 Stihl Br320 / 1 Stihl Br340 bp

- 6.5 x 16 open trailer

How much will it cost to obtain this equipment?

- I already own it.

Where will you store the equipment?

- My garage.

How much will it cost to store the equipment?

- $0.00

Advertising / Promotion:

How will you advertise or promote your business?

- Yellow pages, internet, business cards, post cards, fliers, doorhangers

How much will you spend doing each per year?

- $3,000

Steve: "Can you give us some insight into the following questions. 1. A total number of new customers you feel you can **easily** attract this season.

2. A total number of new customers you feel will be **moderately difficult** to attract this season.

3. A total number of new customers you feel will be **extremely**

tough to attract this season.

4. What date do you want these total customers by?"

Jeff: "1. A total number of new customers you feel you can easily attract this season - 20
2. A total number of new customers you feel will be moderately difficult to attract this season - 30
3. A total number of new customers you feel will be extremely tough to attract this season - 50
I hope to have this many new costumers by September 12th.

I have my set salary at $500 per week and my employee is at $300."

Steve: "How many billable hours do you plan on working each month of this year?"

Jeff: "Jan total billable hours = 20
Feb =30
Mar = 240
Apr =320
May = 320
Jun = 320
Jul = 320
Aug = 320
Sept = 320
Oct = 320
Nov = 200
Dec = 150

Yearly total billable hours = 3080."

Steve: "Here is a customer goal chart for this year ending in August to help motivate you. Now that we have these goals, we will be able to chart your progress throughout the season.

What do you want to bill per hour for your labor?"

Jeff: "$40-60 per hour."

Steve: "Here is a pie chart showing your monthly expenses minus labor. "

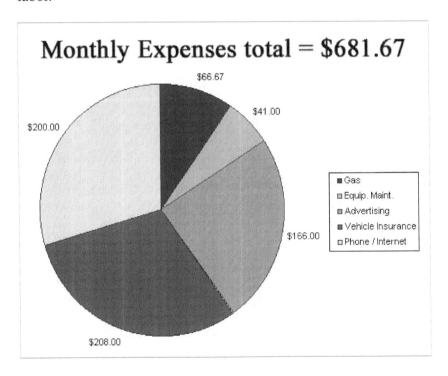

Monthly Expenses total = $681.67

- Gas
- Equip. Maint.
- Advertising
- Vehicle Insurance
- Phone / Internet

Jeff: "The next thing that I am doing is going to be advertising in the yellow pages. I really haven't distributed a great amount of flyers yet. I have been mostly using business cards. My business has doubled since last year at this time. Not in size but in income and profit. I plan on hiring another guy real soon. Thank you for your help! I have learned a lot."

Project: Pro Lawn Services

Joe: "I am starting in the biz full time this year. I have been working on this biz for approx 3 months now (Full Time).

I left a job 3 months ago making reaaaallllly good cash (6 figures). It was one of those safe secure jobs that everyone talks about that really doesn't exist.

A little background, I have been doing lawn care work for approx 5 years when I had time (5 Customers). Last year I got completely out of the biz because I was traveling a lot. I was laid off 3 months ago when the company lost a large federal contract. I decided that I wasn't going back to work for someone else.

I already have a lot of equip.
I have already ordered door hangers.
Just lettered the truck today (Trailer will be done next week)
I got a very basic website up.
I borrowed several logo templates from the free collection at your http://www.gophergraphics.com site and cut & pasted together.

I plan on putting out fliers as listed below.

- 5,000 beginning of March
- 5,000 by March 15
- 2,000 magnetic biz cards by March 31
- 50 12x18 yard signs will be put next to roads leading to developments that I want to service.

Newspaper advert starts on wed this week, will run every wed for 3 months.
I plan on writing articles for the local paper which will be published for free (community service type articles IE: Benefits

of Aeration, Why do we need Lime, Proper way to prune, etc.). These will be published on Wed and will refer to authors AD on page XX.

I have not been able to run demographics on the area's that I am in (They don't drill down to this area).

I will post the logo, truck, and sign pic's. If some of you folk's could provide some feedback, it would be greatly appreciated. If you could help in any way I will be extremely grateful. I am really what you would say betting the farm on this. Failure is not an option since I have basically used up all of my cash reserves or will have by June.

If anyone can find better demographics for my zip code area, it would be a big help.

Here is my business plan."

Business Description:

Give a one paragraph description of your business.

- We are a full service Landscape maintenance company. We provide services for every season. We focus on high maintenance properties located in affluent neighborhoods. We do not attempt to compete on price.

Where is your business located?

What services does your business offer?

- Design / Installation
- Mowing
- Aeration
- Over-seeding / re-seeding
- Sod
- Spring / fall cleanup
- Tree services (contracted out)
- Applications (contracted out)
- Snow / Ice management

What value does it add to the marketplace?

- We are the only company in the area to offer single point of contact for all landscape maintenance needs. In addition, we offer 12 month billing cycles for budgeting purposes

Management Abilities:

What are your qualifications?

- I have been working this business part time for 5 years. I have a masters degree in computer science and 15 years as a federal IT contractor.

How will your experience contribute to the success of your business?

- I am very good at ascertaining a customer's true needs versus their perceived needs and steering them in the right direction.
  I am also very well versed in all types of politics from a contractor's standpoint. (This will serve well when bidding on commercial contracts).

Business Strategy:

What are the key strategic opportunities you have identified in your marketplace?

- This area is a boaters paradise, There are a lot of summer vacation homes in this area.

How will your business take advantage of these strategic opportunities more effectively than your competition?

- I have always focused on providing services for the vacation homes, This will continue to be my primary target. The customers want no excuses for the properties not being done. I provide better than average quality and on-time delivery. Most of these properties are owned by out of state businesses, so they should be really receptive to the 12 month billing cycle.

How do you intend to maintain your competitive edge?

- Always providing on time delivery of service (The number one complaint I hear when bidding jobs).

Describe the key challenges you face and how will you overcome them?

- Gaining enough customers to provide enough cash flow for the first year will be the biggest challenge. I have put together what I think is a good marketing plan.

Legal Structure:

Will your business operate as a sole proprietor, partnership, corporation or an LLC?

- Sole Proprietor this year, S-corp, next year, C-corp in three years.

How will your legal structure decrease your business's exposure to risk?

- This year, I will have no protection.

Financial:

How much will you personally invest in your business?

- I have already paid the insurances for the year out of pocket.
  I have already purchased all equipment. Own it

How much money are you seeking from banks?

- None

How much money are you seeking from private investors?

- None

How long until you plan to break even?

- Equipment already paid for itself.

How long until you plan on making a profit?

- This year.

What will your start-up costs be? Be specific, describe each and the cost.

- Insurances (Auto, Gen liability) $4,000.00 already paid
- Advertising $3,000.00 already paid (All materials are waiting to be distributed)
- Trailers / Mowers / Misc. already paid

What is your sales forecast for each month of the entire year? List each month's goal.

- Really can't forecast at this time. I can only list what I absolutely have to have in order to cover expenses. (My salary is also considered an expense.
  May – Dec = $8,500.00 monthly

What will be your operating expenses? Be specific, describe each and the cost.

- Fuel = $600.00 monthly
- Maintenance = $250.00 monthly
- Equipment Replacement = $1,000.00 yearly

What will your fixed costs be? Be specific, describe each and the cost.

- Phone - $100.00 monthly
- General liability insurance - $1,200.00 yearly
- Commercial Auto Rider - $100.00
- Advertising – $300.00 yearly
- Salary – $7,000.00 monthly
- Taxes – $2,100.00 monthly

Mission Statement:

What is your business?

- We provide the best value proposition for all of your lawn and landscape needs throughout all four seasons.

How will your business succeed?

- Maintaining our commitment to quality services and customer service.

What values are important to your business?

- Customer satisfaction.
- Best quality.
- On-time delivery.

How does your business improve the lives of your customers' and employees'?

- We give them their weekends back.

Marketing Slogan:

What is your marketing slogan?

- I really don't have one.

Market Analysis:

- I haven't really done any.

Customer Analysis:

Who are your target customers? (age range, education level, occupations, average home value)

- Most are business owners
- $400,000.00 + home value

What do your customers want?

- On time delivery
- Quality service (Bragging rights, my lawn looks better than yours)

Competition Analysis:

Who are your competitors?

- Most are retired folks with a single mower doing it to supplement income. One large company with 4 crews of 2 ppl each.

How many employees do they have?

- 12-14

What is their estimated sales volume?

- I don't know.

What services do they offer?

- Full Service (They have pest lic.)

What is the quality of their product?

- Nothing special (Mow, Blow, and Go)

What is the price range of their product?

- $40.00 a half acre.

Who are there customers?

- Anyone that calls.

What are their strengths?

- Low prices, full service.

What are their weaknesses?

- No commitment to quality.

Are they a direct or indirect competitor?

- direct

Labor:

How many employees will you start with? Full or p/t?

- Myself and my daughter.

What will the hourly labor wage paid to employees be?

- I need salary of $6,000.00 monthly
- Daughter will be paid $10.00 hourly. (She will work when I need her)

What will your total annual labor hours be?

- Hopefully 60 man hours weekly after the 1st month.

Equipment:

What equipment will be needed?

- Mowers
- Trimmers
- Blowers
- Hand tools
- Truck
- Trailer
- Plow

    Dodge 2500 Diesel (180,000 miles and 560 RWHP)
    Home Made Salt Spreader
    Meyers 7.5 w/pro wings

    28 ft enclosed trailer w/ 5KW genset / Welder / torches / Air Condition / Fridge

    Kubota GF1800 (60")
    Kubota F2400 (72")
    21" Honda
    Echo Backpacks (2)
    Echo Line Trimmers (2)
    48" Core Aerator
    48" spike Aerator

48" lawn roller
Honda ATV

How much will it cost to obtain this equipment?

- $0.00

Where will you store the equipment?

- Enclosed trailer at residence

How much will it cost to store the equipment?

- $0.00

Advertising / Promotion:

How will you advertise or promote your business?

- Newspaper (Currently running)
- Door Hangers
- Post it notes
- Bus cards
- Yard Signs
- Truck / Trailer lettering
- Word of mouth

How much will you spend doing each per year?

- Newspaper (Currently running) $2,000.00
- Door Hangers $700.00
- Post it notes $200.00
- Bus cards $200.00
- Yard Signs = $400.00

- Truck / Trailer lettering

Steve: "What are your customer projections?

1. A total number of new customers you feel you can **easily** attract this season.

2. A total number of new customers you feel will be **moderately difficult** to attract this season.

3. A total number of new customers you feel will be **extremely tough** to attract this season.

4. What date do you want these total customers by?"

Joe: "I believe that 30 customers would be fairly easy to do, 50 would be moderate and 100 difficult.

I would like to see 70 customers by June 30 even though we are currently in early March."

Steve: "How many billable hours are you projecting for each month?"

Joe: "That is going to totally depend on the number of customers. I would say that we would be capable of working an average of 240 man hours per month allowing for weather related issues. I am figuring Dec, Jan, Feb will be slower. I am trying to estimate jobs at close to $50.00 per man hour."

Steve: "Here is a chart to show your customer goals for this season.

The easy goal is charted to attain the lower level of your easy goal, 30 new customers.

The moderately difficult goal is charted to attain the middle of your moderately difficult goal, 50 new customers.

The extremely tough goal is charted to attain the high end of your extremely tough goal, 70 new customers."

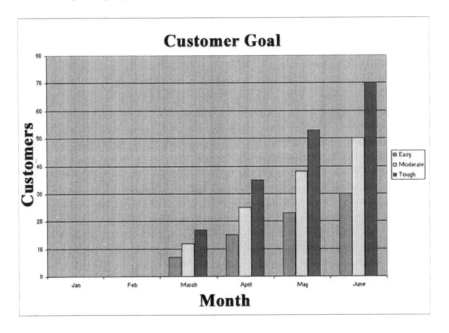

Joe: "Based on my marketing approach, what do you feel the likelihood of me picking up 70 accounts would be for this year?"

Steve: "I think it is possible. It will be tough though. Your goal is one of the most ambitious we have seen so far. This means to achieve it you will have to work harder and smarter than most others.

Something you might want to consider is to pick a day every week that you are out marketing. Think about how local politicians market themselves. They go door to door and meet as many people as possible. Then they hand out flyers and or a magnetic business card to remember them. In your flyer you can have a written in date that a special will be available until. Suggest different services you notice the home owner's yard could use. Meet as many people as possible. The more you meet, the more will see how they interact with you and want you to perform the services over a competitor."

Project: A Plus Landscape & Lawn Care

Tom: "A Plus Landscape and Lawn Care is a single man operation, two-man when needed. We offer expert grass cutting, pruning, planting, and residential landscape installation. Unlike other companies who may have employees "just doing a job", we have an obsession with perfection and doing things the way we would have them done for us. Almost five years of golf course and landscape management has given me the confidence and know-how to start my own business.

Services offered:

- grass cutting
- pruning
- planting
- chainsaw work
- pressure washing
- gutter cleaning
- general handy man / minor home repairs
- general carpentry

I would like to have 2,000 man hours annually with 1 man and a 2 week vacation.

I currently have 5 houses I maintain and some other odd jobs that pop up every once in a while.

I have about $8k in equipment and hope to have it all paid off before the end of the season. I'd like to pick up about 20 or so new customers this year, but I think it might just be difficult to do so.

Monthly expenses:

- equipment $300
- maintenance $40
- gas $100
- advertising $15
- cell phone $45
- insurance health/ liability $120

Maybe $620? something like that per month.

Marketing:

I will utilize word of mouth advertising, business cards, magnetic signs on truck, flyers.

Equipment List:

- 21" honda hrx w/ hydrostat tranny
- 48" exmark metro hp
- stihl fs250r trimmer
- echo 403t blower
- echo 150 hedge trimmer"

I'm not sure I know much about marketing strategy and analysis. I guess I'm just going to bust my butt to do everything in such a way that competitors will have a hard time matching my quality. I don't really care who my customers are as long as they pay me. They all live in or around my area. I'd like to have only millionaires as customers so I could charge them enormous amounts of money for perfection, but that's not a reasonable thought right now. The competitors are the same here as every where else, a few huge companies with many crews and disgruntled employees who do the bare minimum to keep their job. A few established guys who do a great job and have full customer lists, and the low baller guys who half-ass everything. I'm trying to get to the point where I'm one of the guys who does a great job and has the full customer list."

Steve: "I see you want to have a total of 2,000 man hours for the year. How many billable hours do you plan on working **each month** of this year? Because your seasons will change, they may effect your workload based on the services you provide.

Jan total billable hours =
Feb =
Mar =
Apr =
May =
Jun =
Jul =
Aug =
Sept =
Oct =
Nov =
Dec =

Yearly total billable hours = 2,000

Also what is your goal to bill per man hour?"

Tom: "Maybe it would be a good start to shoot for this

- Jan= 80 hrs
- Feb= 100 hrs
- Mar=120 hrs
- Apr=160 hrs
- May=160 hrs

- July=160 hrs
- Aug=160 hrs
- Sept=160 hrs
- Oct=120 hrs
- Nov=100 hrs
- Dec= 80 hrs

1,400 total billable hrs.

I will try to get $20/ hr for labor, but I would like to get $30/ hr just labor no other costs figured in."

Steve: "Here is a pie chart that shows your annual expenses."

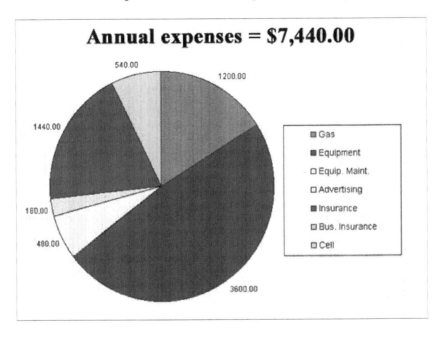

Project: Bill's Lawns

Bill: "Here is my business plan.

Business Description:

Give a one paragraph description of your business.

- Our business is a lawn/home maintenance service.

What services does your business offer?

- Mowing
- Blowing
- Mulch Installs
- De-thatching
- Edging etc
- Also small repairs and landscape maintenance.

What value does it add to the marketplace?

- Local, young company, identifiable by most in the area.
- Flexibility on services and time.

Management Abilities:

What are your qualifications?

- Our qualifications are a combined 25+ years of landscaping and maintenance experience. We are all active and physically fit people. I myself hold a degree in Sports Management, and a minor in Communications. At some point, we have all worked in the field, in both the residential and commercial segments. We all have experience in customer service, as a professional athlete, in the gaming industry, and retail sales.

How will your experience contribute to the success of your business?

- Between the three of us, we can take care of the management facets, such as marketing/sales, labor/onsite, and financial.

Business Strategy:

What is your business strategy?

- Creating residential and commercial volume through a model of low cost strategy. (My overhead is very inexpensive.)

What are the strengths of your business strategy?

- The area is full of overpriced franchise types, that care little about the end product or the customer.

What are the weaknesses of your business strategy?

- I really do not see any if we stick to the business model, although we may lose potential customers that will stick with the status quo.

What are the key strategic opportunities you have identified in your marketplace?

- We have a close tie in to the real estate market in the area, and as it is a growing area, it provides a tremendous foot in the door. There are many new residential and commercial developments in the area.

How will your business take advantage of these strategic opportunities more effectively than your competition?

- Well, simply put, we seem much more connected to those in the area then the larger businesses.

How do you intend to maintain your competitive edge?

- Keep networking, community efforts, signage, publicity etc.

Describe the key challenges you face and how will you overcome them?

- We are a startup business with very little reputation for the industry we are in for this area.

Legal Structure:

Will your business operate as a sole proprietor, partnership, corporation or an LLC?

- Partnership evolving into a LLC

How will your legal structure decrease your business's exposure to risk?

- It won't until we file our papers.

Financial:

- I need more time to figure some parts out still.

How much will you personally invest in your business?

- $4,000

How much money are you seeking from banks?

- None

How much money are you seeking from private investors?

- None

How long until you plan to break even?

- About two months or so.

How long until you plan on making a profit?

- About 4 months.

What will your start-up costs be? Be specific, describe each and the cost. Still trying to figure that out.

- It seems that at minimum it will be $4,000.

What is your sales forecast for each month of the entire year? List each month's goal.

- What will be your monthly operating expenses? Be specific, describe each and the cost.

What will your monthly fixed costs be? Be specific, describe each and the cost.

- Insurance, license, gas & fuel, promotion, web fees (e-mail, hosting), to name a few.

Mission Statement:

What is your business?

- Lawn and Landscape Maintenance.

How will your business succeed?

- Hard work, proper management and being fiscally responsible.

What values are important to your business?

- Dependability, Integrity, Quality are key for us.

How does your business improve the lives of your customers' and employees'?

- We provide employment opportunities for local youth, which have proven to give back to the community in other areas. We also give people a chance to not worry so much about the yard, and upkeep and concentrate on other areas of life.

Marketing Slogan:

What is your marketing slogan?

- Haven't come up with one I truly like.

Market Analysis:

What are the positive NATIONAL trends that will affect your business?

- Disposable income of the baby boomer generation, and the push to enjoy more "quality" time.

What are the negative NATIONAL trends that will affect your business?

- Gas and fuel prices are sky high, We are taxed beyond belief.

How will you take advantage of the positive trends and deal with the negative trends?

- Sell our services and business to all those baby boomers by volume.

What are the positive REGIONAL trends that will affect your business?

- We live in an area with with retirees.

What are the negative REGIONAL trends that will affect your business?

- SNOW, small population, and oh yeah did I mention snow?

How will you take advantage of the positive trends and deal with the negative trends?

- Most retirees want to feel appreciated and known. Our personalities will carry us. As for the snow? Pray?

What are the positive LANDSCAPE INDUSTRY trends that will affect your business?

What are the negative LANDSCAPE INDUSTRY trends that will affect your business?

How will you take advantage of the positive trends and deal with the negative trends?

Customer Analysis:

What is your current customer base?

- About 5 lawn care accounts.

Who are your target customers? (age range, education level, occupations, average home value)

- Baby boomers, and cottagers, there is a wide range for ages, levels of education etc.

What do your customers want?

- Service that is reliable, and quality

Competition Analysis:

Who are your competitors?

- Everyone, even the big guys (lawn maintenance anyway).

How many employees do they have?

- It varies from solo operators to crews.

What is their estimated sales volume?

- More than me..I really haven't been able to find that info.

What services do they offer?

- Varies, some are licensed to use pesticides.

What is the quality of their product?

- It ranges from horrible to ok.

What is the price range of their product?

- $15 a cut and up.

Who are there customers?

- Same as the ones I am targeting.

What are their strengths?

- They are franchised for the most part, with a strong backbone to rely on.

What are their weaknesses?

- They are cold to their customers.

Are they a direct or indirect competitor?

- Direct.

Equipment:

What equipment will be needed?

- We have it all already

How much will it cost to obtain this equipment?

- Nothing

Where will you store the equipment?

- In my garage.

How much will it cost to store the equipment?

- Nothing

Advertising / Promotion:

How will you advertise or promote your business?

- Word of mouth, local media, website, brochures, networking.

How much will you spend doing each per year?

- To be determined.

Steve: "What are the total number of new customers you feel you can **easily** attract this season.

2. A total number of new customers you feel will be **moderately difficult** to attract this season.

3. A total number of new customers you feel will be **extremely tough** to attract this season.

4. What date do you want these total customers by?"

Bill: "We have 5 customers already. They are small, but they are ours.

I think we can attract at least 15 more easily.

25 moderately

45 extreme

I would like these total customers by May 1 and it currently is the end of March."

Steve: "How many billable hours do you plan on working each month of this year?"

Bill: "Jan total billable hours = 0
Feb = 0
Mar = 0
Apr = 240
May = 240
Jun = 240
Jul = 240
Aug = 240

Sept = 240
Oct = 240
Nov = 160
Dec = 0

Yearly total billable hours = 1,840

I am using these figures as a minimum. I am looking more toward 3,000 hours as a high depending on how my sales go.

As far as how much I would like to bill for these hours, I really do not know how to answer that question. How much I want to make, is going to really depend on my fixed costs, and what service(s) I am billing for.

I made some adjustments to some of my costs.

- Gas: $300.00
- Maintenance of equipment $75.00
- Regular Advertising: $100.00
- Office Supplies: $50

The monthly fixed costs are:

- Truck: $0
- Insurance: $340
- Bus. Insurance: $62.00
- Plow: $0
- Phone, Internet: $75.00
- Cell: $120.00

I am going to be handing out some flyers in my area soon with three different coupons on them. The left coupon says 10% off lawn services with prepay. The middle says 15% off Spring clean up with seasonal lawn care package and the right says 10% off any services $400 or more."

Project: Western Lawn

Jerry: "This is my business plan for my lawn care business.

Business Description:

Give a one paragraph description of your business.

- We provide all-in-1 lawn care service for less.

What services does your business offer?

- We currently offer: Lawn Mowing, Shrub & Hedge Trimming, Small Tree Trimming and Removal up to 7', Brush Clearing, Leaf Clean-up, Small Landscaping and Landscape Upgrades. Misc. Yard Clean Up. Fall/Spring Clean Up. Annual color beds, Christmas Decorations.

What value does it add to the marketplace?

- I believe it adds a lot of value when you can get one company to do all you need to your property.

Management Abilities:

What are your qualifications?

- I helped my Mom take care of her 2 acre property since I was 10, then when we moved, I took care of her 1 acre home then. Also my great grandfather had a nursery/landscape design up north and taught my mom all he knew and she taught me.

How will your experience contribute to the success of your business?

- It will give me somewhat an edge over the newbie's but not as much as the seasoned pros.

Business Strategy:

What is your business strategy?

- To buy used equipment to start off. To keep a low overhead and then buy newer equipment with cash when needed or I can.

What are the strengths of your business strategy?

- A low overhead = more profit.

What are the weaknesses of your business strategy?

- Used equipment has a higher chance of breaking down.

What are the key strategic opportunities you have identified in your marketplace?

- I live in the middle of the retirees that can't do their own lawns any more. So that will lead to a higher chance of getting the job.

How will your business take advantage of these strategic opportunities more effectively than your competition?

- We will cater to most of their needs we can fill.

How do you intend to maintain your competitive edge?

- I go to 90% of all trade show each year & get all magazines to stay current on new topics.

Describe the key challenges you face and how will you overcome them?

- Losing the customer to low bidding newbie's. And we should over come them by 1, they don't provide great service. 2, they go out of business from pricing jobs to low.

Legal Structure:

Will your business operate as a sole proprietor, partnership, corporation or an LLC?

- Sole proprietor.

How will your legal structure decrease your business's exposure to risk?

- By being a sole proprietor, I don't have to deal with partners wanting there share or there say in the company.

Financial:

How much will you personally invest in your business?

- $3,000

How much money are you seeking from banks?

- None due to credit issues.

How much money are you seeking from private investors?

- None.

How long until you plan to break even?

- 1 year or less.

How long until you plan on making a profit?

- 1 year or less.

What will your start-up costs be? Be specific, describe each and the cost.

- Trailer $750
- 36" W/b mower $500
- Trailer hitch $150
- Blower $139
- Trimmer/Edger combo $200
- Insurance $429
- License $75

What is your sales forecast for each month of the entire year? List each month's goal.

What will be your monthly operating expenses? Be specific, describe each and the cost.

- Fuel Prices raising and lowering.

What will your monthly fixed costs be? Be specific, describe each and the cost.

- Promotion's (flyers, signup deals), web hosting fees.

Mission Statement:

What is your business?

- Lawn & Landscape Maintenance / Installs

How will your business succeed?

- Attention to detail.

What values are important to your business?

- Quality work & reasonable price's.

How does your business improve the lives of your customers' and employees'?

- I don't know yet.

Marketing Slogan:

What is your marketing slogan?

- At Western Lawn, you get fast, reliable, service, competitive prices, & attention to detail. (may need some work still?)

Market Analysis:

What are the positive NATIONAL trends that will affect your business?

- People want to spend more time with family and enjoy there lawn.

What are the negative NATIONAL trends that will affect your business?

- I don't know.

How will you take advantage of the positive trends and deal with the negative trends?

- I don't know.

What are the positive REGIONAL trends that will affect your business?

- Smaller lawns take less time to finish the work so we can do more in the day.

What are the negative REGIONAL trends that will affect your business?

- The government stepping in with more rules.

How will you take advantage of the positive trends and deal with the negative trends?

- I don't know.

What are the positive LANDSCAPE INDUSTRY trends that will affect your business?

- Drought tolerant plants.

What are the negative LANDSCAPE INDUSTRY trends that will affect your business?

- Hurricanes.

How will you take advantage of the positive trends and deal with the negative trends?

- Plant plants that use less water than the normal plants and try to deal with the weather.

Customer Analysis:

What is your current customer base?

- 3 customers.

Who are your target customers? (age range, education level, occupations, average home value)

- age range, 18-up
- education level, Any
- occupations. everyone but other lawn guys
- average home value, $130,000

What zip codes do they live in?

- Only in my county.

What do your customers want?

- Great service at competitive prices.

Competition Analysis:

Who are your competitors?

- I lost count.

How many employees do they have?

- I don't know.

What is their estimated sales volume?

- I don't know.

What services do they offer?

- Lawns / Landscaping.

What is the quality of their product?

- I don't know.

What is the price range of their product?

- I don't know.

Who are there customers?

- The same as mine.

What are their strengths?

- I don't know.

What are their weaknesses?

- Me.

Are they a direct or indirect competitor?

- Both.

Labor:

How many employees will you start with? Full or p/t?

- None.

What will the hourly labor wage paid to employees be?

- None.

What will your total annual labor hours be?

- Jan total billable hours = 224
- Feb = 224
- Mar = 224
- Apr = 224
- May = 224
- Jun = 224
- Jul = 224
- Aug = 224
- Sept = 224
- Oct =112
- Nov = 224
- Dec = 224

- Yearly total billable hours = 2576

Equipment:

What equipment will be needed?

- 36" Walk behind mower
- 21" Trimmer/Edger
- Blower
- Misc Tools

How much will it cost to obtain this equipment?

Where will you store the equipment?

- Trailer in my yard.

How much will it cost to store the equipment?

- None.

Advertising / Promotion:

How will you advertise or promote your business?

- Flyers & word of mouth.

How much will you spend doing each per year?

- $500 min.

Types of expenses:

Different expenses you will want to include in your business plan.

- I want to include insurance $50 / month
- Gas $100
- Equipment Maintenance $25
- Advertising $50
- Cell Phone $90
- Web Hosting $5
- Office Supplies $15."

Steve: "What are your new customers goals for this year?"

Jerry: "A total number of new customers I feel I can **easily** attract this season. {15}

A total number of new customers I feel will be **moderately difficult** to attract this season. {25}

A total number of new customers I feel will be **extremely tough** to attract this season. {40}

Steve: "What date do you want these total customers by?"

Jerry: "End of July/August. It's currently the beginning of April now."

Joel: "Regarding your expenses... have you considered if you will be spending money on any of the following:

Fertilizers & Other Lawn Treatments
Waste Disposal
Bank Interest & Charges
Truck - Repair & Maintenance

Also:

Is the $100 fuel for your truck, your equipment or both?

What is the $50 insurance for? Truck insurance? Business liability insurance? Workers' Comp or disability insurance? Have you considered the cost of all of these?

Internet Access/Hosting - You put $5 for hosting. What do you pay for internet access (you can write this off too)."

Jerry: "Spending money on any of the following:

Fertilizers & Other Lawn Treatments - I don't do. Too much b.s. to go through to get a license for it.

Waste Disposal - $25 Customer pays it.

Bank Interest & Charges - Free Checking from bank.

Truck - Repair & Maintenance - oil changes every 3 months $25.

Is the $100 fuel for your truck, your equipment or both?

Both so far. All I have is a 21" push, trimmer and edger, blower.

What is the $50 insurance for?

Truck insurance - truck is on personal insurance

Business liability insurance- yes

Workers' Comp or disability insurance- no

Have you considered the cost of all of these? not yet

Internet Access/Hosting - $5 for hosting.

What do you pay for internet access (you can write this off too)?

Comcast online- $42.95 month

MSN for email- $10 month"

Steve: "Here is a chart to show your customer acquisition goals for this year."

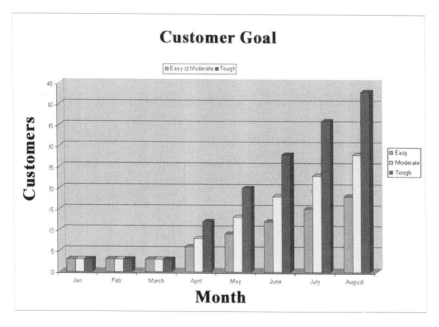

Jerry: "Here is my expected revenue for that month. With the cheapest mowing I do is $145 a month.

- 15 customers would equal $2,175 a month
- 25 customers would equal $3,625 a month

- 40 customers would equal $5,800 a month.

With a monthly revenue of $2,175 and $470 in expenses. My profit would be $1,705 a month.
Later on as I grow, what's good to expand into on other green industry products or services? How can I make more money?"

Joel: "I would suggest providing your existing customers with more services. You mentioned about fertilizing being a bunch of red tape but this can be a high profit service that is probably worth the hassle in the long run. Try to offer your customers full service or you may find them switch to a company that does.

So other than cutting you can offer beds maintenance, trimming and pruning, planting, fertilizing, lawn weed control, lawn specialties such as aeration, lawn renovations/rejuvenations and top dressing.

Keep learning more about horticulture and try to help (and profit) from anything your customer needs for there lawn and garden."

Jerry: "How hard it is to get a Small Business Association Loan for $10,000 for some new equipment?"

Joel: "How hard it is depends on your own situation. Overall, you have to jump through quite a few hoops and you are examined quite thoroughly when you apply for an SBA loam.

Here are the very basic qualifications to get a business loan:

- You must have a reasonable amount already invested in your business.
- Your business plan and other business document must be very detailed. What we have done here is only touching the surface compared to what they will want to see.

- You really need to explain everything about your business, why you need the funds and your plan to pay it back.
- You'll need income statements, balance sheets and long-term forecasts. Lots of paperwork!
- Also, expect to have your personal credit scrutinized (not just the business).
- You will need collateral to secure the loan.

So **you** will have to answer the question as to whether it is worth it or not.

I have not actually known anyone who has got an SBA loan. Most find it too much work to satisfy the eligibility requirements. So I would not recommend this route.

If you are need of capital the easiest type of loan to get is a basic personal loan. You'll still need the collateral but they will not ask for financial statements, forecasts and the like. This is the route that I have used in the past and it is the route I would recommend for Western Lawn and other small/medium sized LCOs if they are in need of capital.

Have you thought about your marketing strategy?

You mentioned some zip codes in your original post but as you are just starting to build up a customer base I think it would be best to focus in a lot more. So you need specific neighborhoods, streets or smaller areas that can targeted with a flyer/doorhanger marketing campaign. These areas do not have to be the nicest areas of town and in fact you are probably better to start in a more middle or upper-middle class area. Keep in mind as well that it may be difficult to get a maintenance agreement from people right away. They want to get to know you first so you may end up doing, perhaps a clean-up or some other service. Once they see what a great job you do they are more inclined to give you more substantial jobs... like the weekly maintenance of the lawn and garden.

So, what I would like you to do is this:

Select at least three specific neighborhoods, streets or smaller areas that are nearby and answer the following questions for each:

> 1) Approx how many houses in this area?

> 2) Why do you like the area? Why does it appeal to you? (i.e. The competition is lousy or lots of seniors who need help... you get the idea)

> 3) What are the demographics of the zip code in which the neighborhood is located. You can do this by checking census records online.

Like this:

Area One
There are approx how many houses?
I like this area because:
The demographics of this area are:

... same for other two.

Take a drive around select some neighborhoods to target.

Another thing is you mentioned getting 5,000 flyers printed, so you have got plenty to get started.

In my opinion the best way to get new customers as you are just starting out is to personally deliver flyers and to talk to as many people as you can. Sure, just dropping the flyers may result in a call or two, but knocking on people's doors, professionally introducing yourself and offering a free quote on the spot (perhaps even offer to do the job the same day if possible) will win people over time and again.

Remember to complement folks on their lawn and garden. Don't slag the competition. Note how you would be able to help them. Do they need a clean-up, some summer color in their beds, some fresh top soil or mulch? Of course, ask for the lawn maintenance too but as I said before, some will want to try you out with something smaller first.

Don't just hit the houses once. Hit them again and again, month after month. Some of your potential customers will see your flyer many times before calling you. It is important to remember that each time a prospect sees your company name they have a little more confidence in you until finally... they have enough to pick up the phone."

Project: Tony's Lawn & Gardens

Tony: "I put together a business plan for my new lawn and garden business and I hope you can help me review it.

What services does your business offer?

- Design / Installation
- Mowing
- Spring / Fall cleanup
- Debris Removal
- Flower bed/landscape renovation

What value does it add to the marketplace?

- We offer competitive services and pricing for our community. We plan to be in this for the long-term, giving a stable source for landscaping and lawn maintenance needs.

Management Abilities:

What are your qualifications?

- I have a degree in interdisciplinary studies, and five years experience as a grade school teacher. In that role, I have experience working for and with large numbers of people, as well as managing large numbers. In addition, I have experience getting a job done with very limited resources.

How will your experience contribute to the success of your business?

- As a teacher, my strength lies in communication. Not only can I listen and ascertain an individual's specific needs, but I can inform and educate to potentially help a client better understand their own needs.

Business Strategy:

What are the key strategic opportunities you have identified in your marketplace?

- The area that I live in is located centrally to three larger communities/cities, one of which is growing at an enormous rate.

How will your business take advantage of these strategic opportunities more effectively than your competition?

- In order to be successful, I intend to expand my business into one or more of these larger communities as I grow and have the ability to do so.

How do you intend to maintain your competitive edge?

- Competitive pricing and top quality service.

Describe the key challenges you face and how will you overcome them?

- Low start-up capital. I plan to grow my business slowly in the beginning, taking on little or no debt. It will grow as I can grow it, and no faster.

Legal Structure:

Will your business operate as a sole proprietor, partnership, corporation or an LLC?

- Sole Proprietor in the beginning, LLC or S-corp as I grow into the need.

How will your legal structure decrease your business's exposure to risk?

- I purchased a one million dollar liability policy.

Financial:

How much will you personally invest in your business?

- I have been paying insurance out of pocket, and have invested in the initial equipment. I have a truck, mower, and trimmer as well as assorted hand tools. I do not yet have a trailer, and I load my mower in the truck bed. I will invest in a trailer when I can pay cash.

How much money are you seeking from banks?

- None.

How much money are you seeking from private investors?

- None.

How long until you plan to break even?

- This year.

How long until you plan on making a profit?

- This year or next.

What will your start-up costs be? Be specific, describe each and the cost.

- Insurances (Auto, Gen liability) approximately $1,000.00.
- Advertising $500.00 already paid.
- Equipment $3,000.00 Already paid.

What is your sales forecast for each month of the entire year? List each month's goal.

- Can't forecast at this time. Currently I have less than $400/month contracted, but I have done around $1,000/month in miscellaneous landscaping jobs the first two months.

What will be your operating expenses? Be specific, describe each and the cost.

- Fuel = $200.00/month
- Maintenance = $50.00/month
- Saving for expansion = variable, as able

What will your fixed costs be? Be specific, describe each and the cost.

- Phone – $45.00
- General Liability Ins – $500.00
- Commercial Auto – $400.00
- Advertising – $700.00

Mission Statement:

What is your business?

- We offer top quality lawn and landscape care.

How will your business succeed?

- Personal attention to each customer; every phone call returned, every concern addressed.

What values are important to your business?

- Quality service.
- Meeting the customer's needs.

How does your business improve the lives of your customers' and employees'?

- We free time that they can better use.

Marketing Slogan:

What is your marketing slogan?

- "What could you be doing if you weren't mowing?"

Market Analysis:

Rural community in close proximity to rapidly growing college town and two other small cities.

Customer Analysis:

Who are your target customers? (age range, education level, occupations, average home value)

- Middle age, upper middle income families with more to do than time to do it.

What zip codes do they live in?

- ??

What do your customers want?

- A property that "keeps up with the Joneses"

Competition Analysis:

Who are your competitors?

- Three large companies in my own community as well as the normal assortment of "here today, gone tomorrow" (I hope) companies. One small company that is to be reckoned with.

How many employees do they have?

- I do not know.

What is their estimated sales volume?

- I do not know

What services do they offer?

- Full Service.
- At least one of these has a chemical applicator's license, or at least I assume they have it as they do applications.

What is the quality of their product?

- One is excellent, one is below average, one I cannot say. The small company mentioned is absolute highest quality, and while I believe that I can match it, I do not believe anyone can beat it. It's what I would want for my own property.

What is the price range of their product?

- $40.00 per acre to mow.

Who are their customers?

- Anyone that calls.

What are their strengths?

- Full service.

What are their weaknesses?

- Price for all, quality for one.

Are they a direct or indirect competitor?

- Direct.

Labor:

How many employees will you start with? Full or p/t?

- Myself and my wife.

What will the hourly labor wage paid to employees be?

- I work for what profit I can turn, as does my wife.

What will your total annual labor hours be?

- Depends on how fast I grow. Currently less than ten per week.

Equipment:

What equipment will be needed?

- Mowers
- Trimmers
- Blowers
- Hand tools
- Truck
- Trailer
- Skid steer

How much will it cost to obtain this equipment?

- $10,000.00 - $20,000.00

Where will you store the equipment?

- In a barn at my home.

How much will it cost to store the equipment?

- $0.00

Advertising / Promotion:

How will you advertise or promote your business?

- Newspaper
- Door Hangers
- Business cards
- Web site possibly
- Truck / Trailer lettering
- Word of mouth
- Video advertising at local restaurant

How much will you spend doing each per year?

Approximately

- Newspaper $300.00-$500.00
- Door Hangers $100-$500
- Bus cards $100.00
- Web site $20.00
- Truck / Trailer lettering
- Word of mouth
- Video $250

Everything here is a best guess, and some things represent ideas rather than die hard plans. The future equipment will depend entirely on how fast I can grow. I have one company that has spoken to me about subbing jobs if I can get/rent a skid steer with a harely rake."

Joel: "Well done with your business plan so far! I was

particularly impressed with your emphasis on good communication which is definitely a key to success. As well, you seem to have taken a look at your competition and are confident about going head-to-head with them. I did have a couple points that I would like to see expanded.

1) You mentioned 3 larger communities in your area. Do you plan on serving all three and if so, will your plan of attack be to market yourself in all three at once?

Without knowing the details of these communities, I would be inclined to take a closer look and perhaps narrow your market, at least in the beginning. In my experience targeting specific neighborhoods in the beginning is a great way to get your foot in the door, build some confidence and then spread your business. So, take another look at your proposed area and try to come up with the top **3 zip codes**. That is, if you were to narrow your market what three zip codes would you choose. With the zip codes you can do some more market research and with demographic information that will help as you target your market.

2) Your competitive advantage. It is really important that you are able to somehow stand out from your competition. You mentioned that you feel your work would be better than most and this of course is a great start. You also mentioned competitive pricing which, if you are starting out, should be a given. Can you think of any other ways to stand out. Something you do particularly well... perhaps a specialty? Anything you come up with will help you greatly as you market yourself. Here are a few examples:

- Extraordinary attention to detail.
- Specializing in lawn repair and rejuvenation.
- Specializing in environmental friendly solutions for lawn and garden.
- Consistently exceed the expectations of your customers."

Tony: "At the moment, it is beginning to look to me like my only advantage is the fact that I do have time to call back customers and give great detail to customer service.

The majority of properties are large, an acre or so in many cases, though there are smaller ones in the townships."

Joel: "Be careful if the areas you want to service are quite far apart. If you must go this distance to get work then I suppose you will have to, but as I mentioned in my previous post it is best if you can target certain areas. Remember, with the price of gas that 'windshield time' can cost you, so I would start with areas that are close together. Once you have selected some areas, your best bet is to hit them again and again with your advertising - not just once.

As you are starting out take even the small jobs as they can lead to much better jobs in the future. Take advantage of your competitive advantage and do a fantastic job and you will soon find your business growing.

Whatever you decide make sure you document your plan. If you decide on this business model it will change your strategies considerably so taking the time to think it through completely will be of great value!"

Project: Pro Turf

Dennis: "I'm new to the lawn care business. I am a detailed person who is passionate about what I do. It boils down to wanting to be the best at what I do and doing whatever it takes to get there.

My goals with my new lawn care business are to provide top notch service to my surrounding area. Don't get me wrong, there are a few companies in my area already doing this, however, after speaking with many homeowners, these big companies lack an agronomically educated individual calling the shots and knowing what's best for a given grass.

I would also like to franchise my business. Why do I want to franchise? Before I can answer this, I must state the mission statement of the business: To provide reliable, affordable, professional lawn care solutions to customers.

Reliable service is a huge factor in this business. Do you care enough about your customers property to make it shine? Will you mow it twice in one week if you have to? Can you keep and maintain a sound maintenance schedule? Do you present a professional image in all aspects of what your doing? Do you respect the money of your customers? I do, I can, and I will! This ties it together pretty well. Many companies offer a lot of services but perform them in blue jeans and tank tops, NOT ME. Many people can't confidently answer routine "grass related" questions, I do and can. If someone were to do work in or around my home, I would much rather a clean, professional looking individual versus a "grimy" looking one. All of my customers love the fact that I am reliable, knowledgeable, honest, and professional.

Ok, so it seems like people really like what I have to offer, why re-invent the wheel? This is what people need, and this is what people want. Everyone needs a reliable, knowledgeable, honest and professional lawn care provider. More importantly, everyone wants their property to stand out. It's a winning combination.

I plan on keeping my expenses lower by doing my homework while maintaining an ever growing network group. I consider myself a people person and I have benefited from this personality trait time and time again. Ex. Today I received free Season Greetings cards that I will have my business name printed on and sent to respected customers. This was the result of a call made to follow up on a faxed estimate. I asked about their career (people LOVE talking about themselves) and learned they print custom stationary/cards. You get the picture.

Being open minded allows many more options to come your way. Phone calls are cheap, call around and see who has better deals on certain products. Stop in and "schmooze" make them remember you! By adopting this mentality, I feel I can have an upper edge on on the competition. A structured operation will also aid in minimal expenses. For example: If I run low on seed, I call my local service rep and have more delivered, possibly to the job site itself. Don't stray away from what works.

Many people go into business with no intention other than making money fast. While doing this, they "keep" so much $$ for themselves they have to keep a higher premium to support their now "fun" lifestyle. GREED GREED GREED. My intention is obviously to make money, however, I would like to provide everyone with a product they can afford, not just the wealthy. Good things come to those who wait, SO DOES $$.

Competing against a startup will likely occur. My established business name and product will help a great deal in terms of competing. If "our" prices are close, why would anyone choose a smaller company versus an established one? I wouldn't!!

Additional services will consist of fertilization, weed treatment/control, and the like. It is easier for the homeowner to pay one company for everything versus one for mowing, another for fertilization, and yet for aerating, and so on. Checks are expensive! For this reason, an applicators license will need to be obtained and kept up-to-date. Either by each individual or by the "owner" or something along those lines.

How will I stand out? Professionalism, Professionalism, Shiny red trucks with green and black logos, always clean. Uniforms, excellent product, customer satisfaction, and afford ability

How will I profit? In large sums (LOL)."

Steve: "Well good for you it seems you really want to do this. Have you put together your business plan yet?"

Dennis: "Here is my business plan.

Mission Statement:

- To provide reliable, affordable, professional lawn care solutions to customers.

Summary of Business:

- Pro Turf is a lawn care provider, specializing in high end lawn care. Our reputation will be built from quality service, educated field technicians, professional client relationships, professional image, and honest workmanship. Our goal is to provide clients with the healthy, picturesque, maintenance free lawn they deserve.

Legal Structure:

- Pro Turf is currently set up as a sole proprietorship. I am currently working on forming a Limited Liability Corporation (LLC).

Customer Analysis:

- Pro Turf will be targeting residential homes in mid-to-high income neighborhoods. These neighborhoods range from developments to suburban areas.

  Most residents will be targeted as customers. This population consists of new homeowners to established ones, young professionals to retiring ones, as well as college graduates and alumni. If done the correct way, many of these people can be converted to Pro Turf customers.

Competition Analysis:

- There are a few main competitors in the area. They range from a one-man operation to multi-crew outfits producing annual numbers from $100,000 upward per season. Services offered by these companies include lawn care, lawn installation, landscaping, and chemical treatments as well as snow plowing. Through experience and question asking, I have learned what my local market will bare in terms of the above mentioned services. The main strengths of the competition are proper equipment for the job, the ability to hire laborers, and capital for advertising.

The major weaknesses of the competition are uneducated field technicians and management personnel, customer attention lacks, professional image is non-existent, and attention to detail on the job is non-existent. I have become familiar with the previously mentioned through speaking with homeowners and observing first hand the quality of work put forth by these companies.

Pro Turf has a Turfgrass Scientist on staff that is well educated in all aspects of lawn care. Employees will be well trained and have numerous opportunities for continuing education in the form of conferences, seminars, and other pertinent classes. Customers are and will be treated as people, not numbers or pit-stops. They will be kept informed and educated on the care of their lawn.

- Newsletters will be sent bi-monthly to all clients to add a personal touch. Collared company shirts, khaki pants, professional proposals and invoices will help promote a professional image. Clean, up-to-date equipment and vehicles will also be a huge factor contributing to the professionalism of Pro Turf. Since attention to detail is a huge part of Pro Turf, extra effort will be made while servicing a lawn to ensure garbage is not mowed over; toys are not destroyed, and no blade of grass left uncut.

Pro Turf will separate itself from the rest by providing reliable, affordable, professional lawn care solutions to customers. Referral programs will also aid in our growth. Discounted rates may apply to customers that show longevity to the company or encourage the use of Pro Turf to friends, family, and neighbors.

The intentions of the business are to be the top service and quality provider in the area. This will easily be achieved by offering the best in lawn care service. From educated personnel to state-of-the-art equipment to distinguished professionalism, Pro Turf will rapidly become the leader in service. Quality is as important as the service itself. Through detailed and informative training sessions, personnel will become familiar with procedures in properly detailing a customer's property. Debris will be cleared from driveways and other walkways, garbage will be pick up and removed, all pertinent areas will be serviced to the highest standard of both the homeowner and Pro Turf leaving a picturesque, maintenance free lawn.

Management:

- I have obtained a vast knowledge of turfgrass management skills from 8 years of employment at high end country clubs. During this time, I learned about growing healthy grass, handling million dollar budgets, crew management, and the type of leader I am. This hands-on experience coupled with my baccalaureate degree from a State University in Turfgrass Management has provided me with the knowledge to confidently make agronomic decisions, and converse with customers. After speaking with many potential clients as well as existing ones', it has come to my attention that the area is in need of an educated lawn care provider. This will play a huge role in the success of Pro Turf.

Business Strategy:

- Positive national trends that may affect Pro Turf are the

ever-growing desire to live in the United States of America. People from countries worldwide are flocking to the USA at a tremendous rate. All of these people/families may be viewed as potential customers. More and more people are using the internet for research and shopping needs. With the aid of a company website, there is a greater chance of being recognized both locally and nationally. A professional website will be a huge benefit to our success.

There are also negative trends that may affect Pro Turf. The unpredictable price of gasoline along with other fluctuating prices such as petroleum based products will cause companies to adjust prices accordingly or absorb the difference.

To take advantage of price fluctuations, Pro Turf will have a firm Terms and Agreement policy. This will cover any and all likely possibilities such as additional surcharges for the rise in gasoline or other related property maintenance products such as fertilizer and weed control products.

Moving on, there are also positive regional trends that will affect Pro Turf. The business is based in a continuously expanding demographic area. Northern cities are encroaching from the north while southern cities are moving northward. This means more potential customers on a local basis.

Of course there are negative trends that will affect the business as well. Real estate is in high demand as a result of the aforementioned. Property is expensive as are the homes located on it or to be built. This leaves less money for the homeowner to spend on lawn care. However, most people are compelled to have something as good as or better than the neighbor. For this reason, a high profile lawn care provider such as Pro Turf will be called to handle the service.

Homeowners want their lawn to look great. More often then not, they lack the time, equipment, knowledge, or desire to do it themselves. For this reason, more and more people are turning to professional outfits to handle such needs. It may be as simple as hanging drywall, fixing a leak, installing a new receptacle, or in our case, lawn care. New homeowners are becoming younger and younger compared to the past. 25-year old professional are seeking good rate on mortgages for their first home. This means more potential customers. It is the years of the early career when the professional is the most eager which equals more work which equals less time to maintain their lawn which means call Pro Turf.

Yes, there are also negative trends that will affect the business. More and more people are becoming their own boss by pulling a trailer of maintenance equipment around and cutting grass. You can see them at every red light with chewing tobacco in their mouth. These are the people that will beat your price by ten dollars to gain a customer. What they lack is a clean appearance, professionalism, education, and a desire to grow their operation. Pro Turf will capitalize on this by upholding a professional image, continuing to become educated in all aspects of business and agronomy, and having a desire to grow the business into something people can rely on.

Labor:

- I have started the business employing myself as the only full time employee. As of November, it will remain the same way entering the next season. I have pain myself just enough to survive while putting the rest back into the business in terms of equipment and advertising.

  Hourly wages paid to employees will be $8.75 to $10.50 per hour depending on experience and job title. Foreman may receive as much as $12.50 per hour depending on experience.

  Billable hours will be a direct result of early spring advertising as well as word of mouth. The work week should consist of 5 ten-hour mowing days leaving Saturday mornings for maintenance.

Financial:

- As of October, I have invested approximately $12,627.28 in the form of a truck and equipment. I view this as a very small price considering the amount of opportunity it lends. I will be seeking further financial aid from outside lenders and investors.

  The monthly fixed expenses are as follows:

  Monthly Fixed Expenses

- Truck Payment $212.12
- Mower Payment $233.15
- Truck Insurance $95.00
- Cell Phone $85.00

Sum = $625.27

Monthly Operating Expenses

- Gas for Truck $300.00
- Gas for Equipment $40.00
- Office Supplies $40.00
- Advertising $250.00

Sum = $630.00

Total Expenses = $1,255.27

Advertising:

- Pro Turf will establish a customer base through direct mailings, door hangers, business cards, as well as word of mouth. Company vehicles will present a logo to the viewing public, uniforms will promote through company insignias, a website will cover the internet shoppers, and our service will keep Pro Turf in the public eye.

The amount spent on advertising is $114.00 plus per month. The $114.00 covers Yellow Book advertising. Direct mailing will be heavy in the early spring reflecting a cost of close to $1,000.00. This will be done on a bi-weekly basis targeting certain areas more than others. Through research and experience, I have learned it is more beneficial to send mail to one person 6 times versus 6 people 1 time. This is the advertising strategy that will be adopted by Pro Turf.

Further mailings will be made throughout the growing season to promote the business and special offers such as "Refer a Friend", Newsletters, and Promotions. The volume of the aforementioned will be a direct result of early season success."

2

21044751R00074

Made in the USA
Lexington, KY
02 March 2013